Cook!

T0372078

In the morning, you might like to do some cooking. If it is mid-morning, it might be brunch! Let's cook up a brunch of eggs and a fresh melon drink.

Hands need to be scrubbed
Then you will need to get an
adult to help you.

Summer melon drink

You will need:

melon

All melons are good.

plums

fresh mint

some liquid

How to do it:

Step 1: An adult will help to cut the skin off the fresh melon. Cut the melon and plums into chunks.

Step 2: Add the melon, plums and mint to the blender. You can add a little liquid. Mix it up in the blender until there are no lumps.

Step 3: Tip the drink from the jug.

Poached eggs on crumpets

You will need:

eggs

crumpets

butter

How to do it:

Step 1: Fill a pot at the tap. Then bring the pot to the boil. You need an adult to help you here.

Step 2: Crack an egg into a dish.

Step 3: Then tip it into the pot. Add the second egg.

Step 4: Cook the eggs until they are solid.

Step 5: Next you need to cook the crumpets.

Step 6: Put butter on the crumpets.

Step 7: Then top the crumpets with the eggs.

Now all you have to do is
drink and munch it all up!

But then there
are the dishes
to do!

Words to blend

cook	good	drink
peel	need	blender
summer	butter	morning
might	poached	boil
brunch	step	crack
second	munch	lumps
bring	adult	plums

Before reading

Synopsis: Make a summer melon drink and poached eggs on crumpets using the instructions in this book.

Review graphemes/phonemes: oo oo ee er or igh oa oi

Story discussion: Look at the cover and read the title together. Ask: *What do you think we'll find out about in this book? Is it fiction or non-fiction? How do you know?* Briefly talk about some of the main differences between a non-fiction text and a story. (Non-fiction normally gives facts about the world or instructions for doing something. Non-fiction often has photos rather than drawn artwork.)

Link to prior learning: Display a word with adjacent consonants from the story, e.g. *brunch*. Ask the children to put a dot under each single-letter grapheme (*b, r, u, n*) and a line under the digraph (*ch*). Model, if necessary, how to sound out and blend the adjacent consonants together to read the word. Repeat with another word from the story, e.g. *crumpets* and encourage children to sound out and blend the word independently.

Vocabulary check: poached – cooked gently in simmering water

Decoding practice: Display the word *scrubbed*. Focus on the *ed* at the end, and remind children that in some words, these two letters make a /d/ sound at the end of the word. Sound out and blend all through the word: *s-c-r-u-bb-d*.

Tricky word practice: Display the word *have*. Read the word, and ask children to show you the tricky bit (*ve*, which makes the sound /v/). Practise reading and spelling this word.

After reading

Apply learning: Ask: *Do you think the instructions in this book would be easy to follow? Were there any places where you felt it would be useful to have more detail?*

Comprehension

- What ingredients are in the drink?

- What do you have to do with the crumpets?

- What's the last thing you have to do, when you've finished cooking and eating?

Fluency

- Pick a page that most of the group read quite easily. Ask them to reread it with pace and expression. Model how to do this if necessary.

- Encourage children to read one of the pages with instructions. Can they read at a steady pace, making the instructions as easy as possible for their listeners to understand?

- Practise reading the words on page 17.

Tricky words review

you	to	do
be	have	into
there	are	no
they	all	like
some	here	little